P9-DID-824

00000183557248

LAURA INGALLS WILDER
Little House on the Prairie

ILLUSTRATED BY GARTH WILLIAMS

CHILDREN'S STORYTELLERS

Laura Ingalls Wilder

by Christina Leaf

BLASTOFF!
4
READERS

BELLWETHER MEDIA • MINNEAPOLIS, MN

Note to Librarians, Teachers, and Parents:

Blastoff! Readers are carefully developed by literacy experts and combine standards-based content with developmentally appropriate text.

Level 1 provides the most support through repetition of high-frequency words, light text, predictable sentence patterns, and strong visual support.

Level 2 offers early readers a bit more challenge through varied simple sentences, increased text load, and less repetition of high-frequency words.

Level 3 advances early-fluent readers toward fluency through increased text and concept load, less reliance on visuals, longer sentences, and more literary language.

Level 4 builds reading stamina by providing more text per page, increased use of punctuation, greater variation in sentence patterns, and increasingly challenging vocabulary.

Level 5 encourages children to move from "learning to read" to "reading to learn" by providing even more text, varied writing styles, and less familiar topics.

Whichever book is right for your reader, Blastoff! Readers are the perfect books to build confidence and encourage a love of reading that will last a lifetime!

This edition first published in 2016 by Bellwether Media, Inc.

No part of this publication may be reproduced in whole or in part without written permission of the publisher. For information regarding permission, write to Bellwether Media, Inc., Attention: Permissions Department, 5357 Penn Avenue South, Minneapolis, MN 55419.

Library of Congress Cataloging-in-Publication Data

Leaf, Christina.
  Laura Ingalls Wilder / by Christina Leaf.
    pages cm. – (Blastoff! Readers: Children's Storytellers)
  Summary: "Simple text and full-color photographs introduce readers to Laura Ingalls Wilder. Developed by literacy experts for students in kindergarten through third grade"– Provided by publisher.
  Includes bibliographical references and index.
  Audience: Ages 5-8
  Audience: K to grade 3
  ISBN 978-1-62617-269-2 (hardcover: alk. paper)
  1. Wilder, Laura Ingalls, 1867-1957–Juvenile literature. 2. Women pioneers–United States–Biography. 3. Women authors, American–20th century–Juvenile literature. I. Title.
  PS3545.I342Z7624 2016
  813'.52–dc23
  [B]
                                            2015001379

Table of Contents

Laura Ingalls Wilder has long been a favorite children's author. Her stories introduced **generations** of kids to life on the western **frontier**. Young readers love learning about times before inventions like electricity.

The Little House **series** has won many awards. It is an American **classic**!

Laura was born in Wisconsin on February 7, 1867. She lived with her parents and three sisters.

When Laura was young, few people lived in the western United States. Families could build a home almost anywhere. Laura's family moved often to find the best land to farm. They carried their belongings in a **covered wagon**.

! fun fact

During her childhood, Laura lived in Wisconsin, Kansas, Minnesota, Iowa, and South Dakota.

Wisconsin

N
W • E
S

covered
wagon →

Laura's parents

Laura's parents were **pioneers**. For much of Laura's childhood, they lived far from any town. Laura's father farmed and hunted for food. Her mother cooked, cleaned, and sewed. If they could not make or grow something themselves, Laura's father traded furs for it.

At age 18, Laura married Almanzo Wilder. They built a house and worked hard on their farm, just like Laura's parents.

"Every job is good if you do your best and work hard."
Laura Ingalls Wilder

Almanzo Wilder

! fun fact
Laura wore a black dress for her wedding. Since pioneers did not have many sets of clothes, she wore her newest dress.

A Daughter's Help

As a married woman, Laura kept busy. She helped Almanzo with the chores and raised their daughter, Rose.

Rose

In 1894, the family moved from South Dakota to Missouri. The journey took more than a month. Laura passed time by telling Rose about her childhood. She also wrote about their travels.

"There's no great loss without some small gain."
Laura Ingalls Wilder

After Rose was grown, Laura started writing articles for a local newspaper. Within a few years, her popularity had increased. She began writing for other newspapers, too.

Rose was also a writer. She encouraged her mother and gave her tips. With Rose as her editor, Laura completed an **autobiography**. She had planned the project for years.

Laura's writing desk

Publishers were not interested in a **nonfiction** book for adults. However, one suggested she make it into a **fiction** book for children.

Little House in the Big Woods (1932)
Farmer Boy (1933)
Little House on the Prairie (1935)
On the Banks of Plum Creek (1937)
By the Shores of Silver Lake (1939)
The Long Winter (1940)
Little Town on the Prairie (1941)
These Happy Golden Years (1943)
The First Four Years (1971)

fun fact

Laura's autobiography, *Pioneer Girl*, was finally published in 2014.

In 1932, *Little House in the Big Woods* was published. Laura based it mostly on her childhood. People loved it! It sold well and received good **reviews**.

Learning Lessons

In her lifetime, Laura published eight books based on her experiences. The books were some of the first to describe life on the American frontier.

! **fun fact**

Laura was 65 years old when her first book was published.

J3 Wilder FARMER BOY

J2 Wilder LITTLE HOUSE ON THE PRAIRIE

J4 Wilder ON THE BANKS OF PLUM CREEK Har

J5 Wilder BY THE SHORES OF SILVER LAKE Har

J6 Wilder THE LONG WINTER Harper

J7 Wilder LITTLE TOWN ON THE PRAIRIE Harper

J8 Wilder THESE HAPPY GOLDEN YEARS Ha

J31 Wilder THE FIRST FOUR YEARS

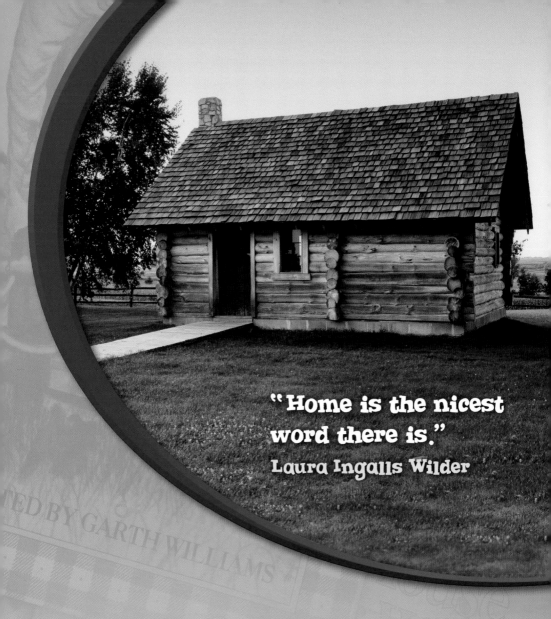

"Home is the nicest word there is."
Laura Ingalls Wilder

Laura's books often focused on the value of hard work. The Ingalls family made most of what they owned, from clothing to houses. They show readers that a simple life can be a happy one.

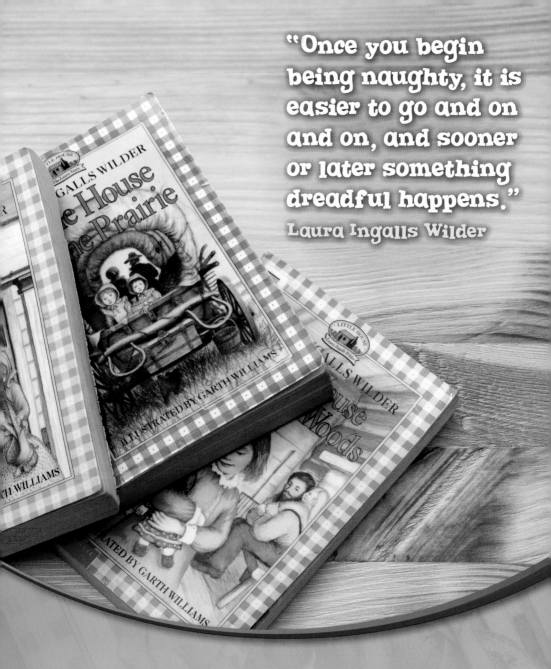

"Once you begin being naughty, it is easier to go and on and on, and sooner or later something dreadful happens."

Laura Ingalls Wilder

Just like her real family, Laura's fictional family is very close. Their **bond** helps them get through tough times.

Sometimes young Laura is naughty in the books. But as she grows older, she sees how this causes trouble for her family. As Laura learns her lessons, young readers learn along with her.

POP CULTURE CONNECTION

In 1974, a television show based on Laura's books first aired. *Little House on the Prairie* focused on the Ingalls' time in Walnut Grove, Minnesota. The popular show ran for nine seasons.

The Little House books are more than 80 years old. But they still delight readers all over the world. Laura won several **Newbery Honors** for her work.

She also had an award named after her. The Wilder Award is given to authors who have a lasting effect on children's writing. It continues to honor Laura's **legacy**.

"Remember me with smiles and laughter, for that is how I will remember you all. If you can only remember me with tears, then don't remember me at all."
Laura Ingalls Wilder

IMPORTANT DATES

1867: Laura is born on February 7 near Pepin, Wisconsin.

1869: The Ingalls family moves to Kansas. This becomes the setting for *Little House on the Prairie*.

1874: The Ingalls family moves to Walnut Grove, Minnesota, which is the setting for *On the Banks of Plum Creek*.

1879: The Ingalls family moves to De Smet, South Dakota. This is the setting for the last five Little House books.

1911: Laura publishes an essay in the *Missouri Ruralist*. She would contribute to this newspaper for years.

1932: *Little House in the Big Woods* is published.

1938: *On the Banks of Plum Creek* is awarded a Newbery Honor.

1943: *These Happy Golden Years* is the last of Laura's books to be published in her lifetime.

1954: Laura receives a new award named in her honor called the Laura Ingalls Wilder Award.

1957: Laura passes away on February 10.

Glossary

autobiography—a biography written by the person it is about

bond—a close connection

classic—a work that will remain popular for a long time because of its excellence

covered wagon—a wagon with an arched canvas top; pioneers traveled in covered wagons to settle new lands.

fiction—written stories about people and events that are not real; Laura's books are fiction because she changed some events and facts about her life.

frontier—an area of open and free land where few people have settled; the western half of the United States was often referred to as the frontier before the Pacific coast was settled.

generations—groups of people who are around the same age at the same time

legacy—the memory or work that a person leaves behind

Newbery Honors—awards given each year to the best American children's books; the Newbery Award is given to first place and the runners-up receive Newbery Honors.

nonfiction—writing that is about facts or real events

pioneers—the first people to move to an area

publishers—companies that make and print books

reviews—articles that discuss the quality of something

series—a number of things that are connected in a certain order

To Learn More

AT THE LIBRARY

Anderson, William. *Pioneer Girl: The Story of Laura Ingalls Wilder*. New York, N.Y.: HarperCollins Publishers, 1998.

Strudwick, Leslie. *Laura Ingalls Wilder*. New York, N.Y.: AV2 by Weigl, 2013.

Wilder, Laura Ingalls. *Little House in the Big Woods*. New York, N.Y.: HarperTrophy, 2004.

ON THE WEB

Learning more about Laura Ingalls Wilder is as easy as 1, 2, 3.

1. Go to www.factsurfer.com.

2. Enter "Laura Ingalls Wilder" into the search box.

3. Click the "Surf" button and you will see a list of related web sites.

With factsurfer.com, finding more information is just a click away.

Index

The images in this book are reproduced through the courtesy of: South Dakota Historical Society/
Wikipedia/ Public Domain, front cover, p. 10 (left); Bellwether Media, front cover (book covers,
background), all interior backgrounds, pp. 5, 15, 18, 21; John Schultz/ Quad-City Times/ ZUMA
Press, pp. 4, 8; Hannah Eckman, p. 7; Wikipedia/ Public Domain, p. 9; Home of Our Fathers/ Public
Domain, p. 10 (right); PorterBriggs/ Public Domain, p. 12; Gayle Harper/ KRT/ Newscom, p. 13; Andre
Jenny Stock Connection Worldwide/ Newscom, pp. 14-15; ZUMA Press, Inc/ Alamy, p. 16; Library of
Congress/ Public Domain, p. 17; Moviestore Collection Ltd/ Alamy, p. 19; Bettman/ Corbis, p. 20.